Saint Paul Winter Carnival
WONDERS

for Edgar...
Happy Wondering!
Kris ☺
Jan. '22

Written by
Kris Haslund

Illustrated by
Sara J Weingartner

BEAVER'S
POND
PRESS

To Anika, Ford and Marta. May you always keep wonder in your heart!
— BAB and JJB

For my Mom and Dad, and for my "little kids," Riley, Georgia, Westen, Elsa,
Adalin, Everett, Emilia, and Eleanor.—KH

To David, because of your endless supply of love and support. —SJW

ISBN: 978-1-59298-831-0

Library of Congress Catalog Number: 2016962062

Printed in the United States of America

First Printing: 2017

20 19 18 17   4 3 2 1

Edited by Angela Wiechmann and Hanna Kjeldbjerg
Book design by Sara Weingartner

To order, visit www.wintercarnival.com

Beaver's Pond Press, Inc.
7108 Ohms Lane
Edina, MN 55439-2129
(952) 829-8818
www.BeaversPondPress.com

BEAVER'S POND PRESS

Printing
provided by

ALLEGRA
DOWNTOWN SAINT PAUL
image360

www.allegrastp.com
Jim Flaherty
Boreas Rex LXXX

Sponsored
by

Bradshaw
Creating Meaningful Events That Celebrate Life®

www.bradshawcares.com
Jason Bradshaw
Boreas Rex LXXXI

In partnership
with

SAINT PAUL
WINTER CARNIVAL

The Coolest Celebration
on Earth

Welcome to the Coolest Celebration on Earth!

Winter Carnival is a very cool time of year, and not just because it is very cold! During the ten days of Winter Carnival the city of Saint Paul comes together as a family to celebrate our city and the special place it is to live, play, and work.

For over 130 years the Winter Carnival has celebrated the traditions and values our city was founded on. Everyone in the city is invited to help play out the story through parades, ice skating, sledding, ice fishing, and all the other winter festivities that were in the mythical story of King Boreas and Vulcanus Rex.

Keeping these traditions is important. Think of it like this—in your family you celebrate holidays, and every family celebrates them a little differently. That's what makes our families unique and special! Winter Carnival is like a ten-day city holiday, where, like a big family, we come together to celebrate Saint Paul's traditions and tell the Winter Carnival story.

Just like Malik, Mai, Ilhan, Louise, Joey, Carlos, and Anika in this book, we all come from different backgrounds and have our own family traditions, but the Winter Carnival is a city tradition we can all share.

Remember the traditions and values you learn in this book, and carry them on to make Saint Paul an even greater city than it is today!

King Boreas LXXXI

Chapter 1

The Legend of the Saint Paul Winter Carnival Begins

There were two activities that Anika loved most in the world. One was going to school with her second-grade friends. The other was hearing Grandpop's stories. Anika was lucky that Grandpop lived at her house. She could see him every day!

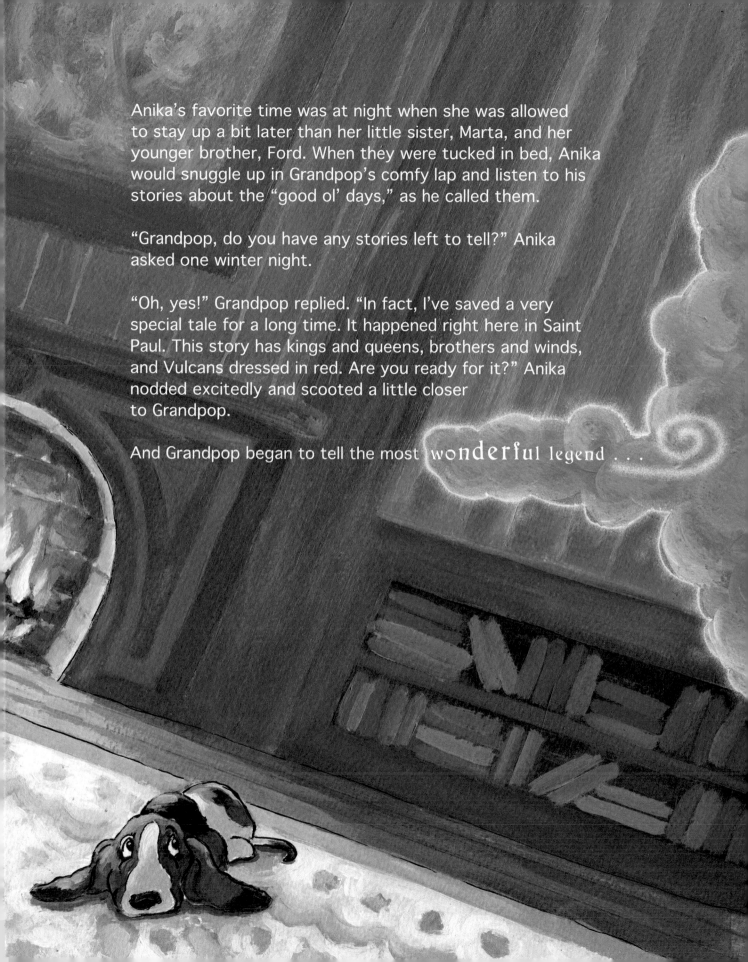

Anika's favorite time was at night when she was allowed
to stay up a bit later than her little sister, Marta, and her
younger brother, Ford. When they were tucked in bed, Anika
would snuggle up in Grandpop's comfy lap and listen to his
stories about the "good ol' days," as he called them.

"Grandpop, do you have any stories left to tell?" Anika
asked one winter night.

"Oh, yes!" Grandpop replied. "In fact, I've saved a very
special tale for a long time. It happened right here in Saint
Paul. This story has kings and queens, brothers and winds,
and Vulcans dressed in red. Are you ready for it?" Anika
nodded excitedly and scooted a little closer
to Grandpop.

And Grandpop began to tell the most wonderful legend . . .

A very long time ago, the goddess of the moon and the god of starlight married on Mount Olympus. They became the parents of five sons. Boreas, the oldest, was given the name "King of the Winds."

"He was the oldest, like me?" Anika interjected. "Then that would make me the Queen of the Winds!"

"Sure," Grandpop agreed. "If Mom and Dad were the moon and stars, then I believe it would be possible!" Grandpop smiled, then continued.

Boreas's first task was to give each of the brothers the power to control one of the winds. So, Titan was chosen as the blustery north wind. Euros, the irresponsible east wind. Zephyrus became the bountiful west wind. And Notos was the balmy but unstable south wind. The four younger brothers played happily over the world's lands and waters.

Boreas often left Olympus and went on long solo journeys. One day, he came upon a beautiful wintery place nestled within seven hills. The place was Saint Paul, Minnesota. He and his queen, Aurora, the Queen of the Snows, would live there. He let the world know that this snowy winter playground would be his new kingdom.

King Boreas wanted to celebrate his
new home. So with the help of his
queen and brothers, he invited people
from each neighborhood of Saint Paul to
his first Winter Carnival.

There were beautiful ice and snow sculptures
throughout the city. Amazing firework displays filled
the night skies. And of course, the Winter Carnival
featured all the city's favorite winter sports.

There were lots of other sports too: curling,
tobogganing, skiing, dogsledding, and even
baseball and golfing in the snow!

King Boreas and the Queen of the Snows lived in the Ice Palace with the Four Wind Brothers and their lovely princesses. From there, the royals ruled over the Winter Carnival for ten days. There was much merrymaking: dancing, feasting, and singing led by Klondike Kate. The royal family and all the city-folk had a splendid time!

Alas, in this land lived a dastardly leader named Vulcanus Rex, the god of fire. He despised seeing winter being celebrated! Vulcanus Rex's bitter plan was to stop Boreas's Winter Carnival with the help of his Fire and Brimstone Krewe.

On the last day of the Winter Carnival, the Vulcans invaded Boreas's Ice Palace. King Boreas did not want to fight the Vulcans. He wanted to protect the city. So upon the good counsel of the Queen, he agreed to compromise. He and the royal family would leave Saint Paul and return to Olympus for most of the year. However, King Boreas and his royal family would come back each year for the Saint Paul Winter Carnival.

And so, we look for their return each year when frosty wintertime rolls around again!

When Grandpop finished telling the legend, Anika's eyes were wide.

"And there's even more to this story," Grandpop said. "They still hold the Saint Paul Winter Carnival, every year. This year's carnival begins next week."

"That sounds really cool!" Anika said excitedly.

"Oh yes!" Grandpop agreed. "In fact, one of the most fun activities is the treasure hunt!" From his pocket, he pulled out seven old coins.

"The Winter Carnival hasn't started yet, but these coins will help you remember this story. Maybe they could even lead you on your very own treasure hunt!" he whispered as he gave them to her.

"Wow," breathed Anika. "A treasure hunt just like at the Winter Carnival?"

"That's right. It's a great mystery full of many wonders. Maybe you can include your friends on the hunt too!"

That night, Anika had a hard time falling asleep. Pictures of King Boreas and his Winter Carnival were still swirling in her head. She couldn't wait for school the next day! She wanted to share the Winter Carnival legend with her best friends.

As for the seven gold coins and the treasure hunt—she would keep that secret for a little while longer!

Chapter 2

Seven Coins, Seven Values, Seven Friends

"You won't believe the story Grandpop told me last night!" Anika exclaimed the next day at recess.

Her friends huddled around her. Anika began to retell the Winter Carnival legend. Mai, Ilhan and Joey wanted to hear more about the royals and the Ice Palace. Malik, Carlos, and Louise especially liked the parts about the Vulcans!

These seven kids had been good buddies since kindergarten. They lived in the same neighborhood, and had already experienced many adventures together.

"I want to learn more about the Winter Carnival tale!" Mai said.

"Yeah," said Joey. "Do you think he would tell us more about it?"

Anika smiled and said, "He sure would!" They made a plan to meet at Anika's house that weekend.

On Saturday morning, the friends
gathered at Anika's, met Grandpop,
and settled down around his chair. The
friends expected him to tell them more
about the legend. They were surprised
when Anika spoke first.

"I've got something to show you!"
she said. She had a twinkle in her eye
and a grin on her face. Her hand was in
her pocket. She gave it a shake.

"Anika, what's making that jingly sound?"
Joey asked curiously.

"Special coins Grandpop gave me!" Anika spread
out the seven old coins for the kids to see.

"Ooh!" and "Ahh!" expressed her astonished friends.

Grandpop reached in and wiped the coins
with an old cleaning cloth. The gold
coins sparkled like new!

The friends carefully studied
the seven coins. They were
very curious about the
symbol and word that
appeared on each.

Anika announced, "Grandpop said that if we figure out what the symbols mean, they will lead us to an amazing treasure!"

"Wow!" and "Cool!" and "Awesome!" her buddies called out.

"I want each of you to have one," Anika continued. "But how will we decide who gets which coin?"

The friends pondered this for a minute. Finally, Malik volunteered, "Let's read the words on the coins. Maybe each word will match up with one of us!"

"Great idea!" Anika agreed. She reached for the first coin. "Okay, this coin says Kindness. I think Mai is very kind. She does many special things for us everyday. So Mai, this one's for you!"

Mai quietly accepted her Kindness coin. She reached for the next coin. "This one says Humility."

"What's that mean?" Joey asked.

"Humility means you don't think you're better than other people," Carlos explained. He was especially good with vocabulary words. "It means you're humble. For example, Ilhan is good in math. But she's very humble about her abilities. She doesn't brag to others."

Joey exclaimed, "So Ilhan should get the Humility coin!"

All the kids nodded in agreement.

"Thanks, guys." Ilhan smiled and reached for a coin. "Hmm . . . Respect."

They all knew what that meant. Respect was their number-one behavior rule at school!

"I think Louise should get that one," suggested Ilhan.

"Yeah," Malik chimed in. "Louise always shows respect! She's the one who taught me about the Golden Rule and treating others the way you want to be treated."

"Thanks, Ilhan and Malik," Louise smiled.

"See—there's that respect again!" Ilhan laughed.

"So who's next?" wondered Louise as she reached for the next coin. "Honesty. I think Joey is really honest. He gave me my field trip money when it dropped out of my locker!"

Joey accepted his coin shyly. "Thanks. Dad taught me honesty is super important!"

Malik picked up the next coin and read, "Generosity."

"I don't get what that means," Joey said.

Carlos replied again, "It's when people are unselfish and understanding. Being generous means you want to give something valuable to people to help or make them happy."

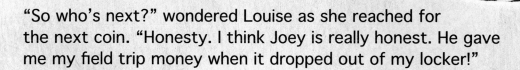

"Well, that's what you are to me, Carlos!" Joey announced. "You're always helping me when I don't understand words."

"That's perfect!" agreed the other friends.

Carlos was pleased to accept the Generosity coin.

"Now there are only two more to go," he said as he picked one. "This next one says Empathy."

Louise was excited. "My mom just taught me that word! It means understanding how other people feel. And that matches with Malik. Even when I'm having a bad day, Malik always knows just what to say to make me feel better."

"For sure!" agreed Ilhan.

"Wow," said Malik. "Thanks! But what about Anika? She's getting stuck with the leftover coin!"

"Don't worry," said Anika. "I'm okay with whatever the last coin says!"

Together, all the friends read aloud, "Gratitude."

"Like how we're all grateful that Anika shared her special coins with us!" suggested Louise.

Anika's friends leapt into the air and shouted a huge, "Thank you, Anika!"

It felt really good to share the old coins. With a gold coin in each of their pockets, they could feel the excitement bubbling through them.

"Are you ready for an adventure?" Grandpop piped in with a smile. "These coins will lead you on your own treasure hunt, just like the real treasure hunt at the Winter Carnival!"

Grandpop then handed Anika a parchment scroll tied with a golden string. Once she unrolled it, the friends quickly realized it was a map that would lead them to the real treasure!

Chapter 3

The Treasure Hunt Adventure

The friends were eager to begin the hunt. They all squished together and carefully studied the drawings on the map.

It took Louise only a minute to notice something.

"Hmm . . ." she said as she pointed to the edge of the map. "This looks like the Saint Paul skyline. And that drawing looks like a swing set. And that's a jungle gym. I think the treasure is hidden on the school's playground!"

The friends jumped up and hugged Louise.

"You are really great at reading maps!" Anika said.

"So let's go!" Joey said.

They giggled and kept bumping into each other as they hurried to the playground. Anika proudly carried the treasure hunt map.

Once they reached the playground, the seven rushed around searching high and low for the treasure.

"Hey! Look over here," called Ilhan.

She discovered an old wooden box taped to the bottom of the slide. The kids took off their mittens and tried to pry the tape from the slide. Before long, the old box lay at their feet. It was heavy.

"Woah! Look at that!" shouted Joey, pointing at the box.

The box was closed shut with a big metal combination lock with a dial. On top of the lid were seven slots. The kids were more determined than ever to discover what was in the treasure chest!

The friends all imagined how they could open the box. Soon, Carlos was standing up laughing. His eyes were focused on the mysterious slots on the box.

"Look! I bet our coins fit into the slots!"

The kids jumped up and high-fived Carlos for being so observant. They each dug into their pockets to grab their coins.

Next it was Joey's turn to shine. He noticed faded words written under each slot. Squinting, the words came into focus.

"Kindness, Humility, Respectfulness, Honesty, Generosity, Empathy, and Gratitude," he read. "These words match our coins!"

The kids all clambered to try their coin first. Mai put her coin in the Kindness slot. It slipped right in. With a ping, a little flag popped up from the slot. Everyone jumped back in surprise, looking at each other and laughing.

Excited, Ilhan slid her coin into the Humility slot. Another ping, another flag!

The rest of the coins were "pinged" into place, and soon there were seven flags sticking out of the box, and each flag had a letter on it. Together the friends saw what word was spelled out.

"WONDERS!" they yelled in unison.

After a moment, Joey spoke up. "So, what does this mean for us?"

The friends all looked at each other, puzzled.

From his view, Carlos could see the back of the flags. Suddenly he noticed that there were numbers on the backsides. He read the numbers out loud: "Five. Two. One. Zero. Two. One. Seven."

Suddenly, Malik whooped with joy. "The numbers must be the combination to the lock!"

The kids took turns spinning the dial to each number. Right to five, left to two, right, left, right, until Anika turned it to the final number and the lock popped open!

Lifting the box's lid, the friends saw their own coins lying at the bottom. They also spied a larger sparkly coin imprinted with a crown.

"Yippee! We found the treasure!" cried out the kids.

"Now what?" Joey piped up. "What does that new coin mean?"

A sharp wind had begun to blow in. "Let's take the box to my house and show Grandpop. He'll know what to do next," Anika decided.

The friends quickly agreed. They took turns carrying the heavy treasure box back down the street. The kids were super excited to tell Grandpop about their discoveries. They hoped that he, in turn, could tell them more about the crown coin. They just knew it had something to do with the Winter Carnival!

Chapter 4

The Wonders of the Winter Carnival

Grandpop welcomed the kids with congratulations, "I'm proud of how well you worked together to find the treasure box and figure out what your coins meant!"

"Thanks!" all seven kids shouted, beaming with smiles, and high-fiving each other.

"You never gave up and solved the problem together." Grandpop added, "You did just as I hoped you would when I created this treasure hunt for you!"

The kids were astonished at Grandpop's news!

"You made this treasure hunt just for us?" Anika asked, her eyes wide.

"Yep!" Grandpop said. "And I have an even bigger secret. Long ago, I played the role of King Boreas at the Winter Carnival. This crown coin was the real one I had designed for my reign!"

"Wow!" the kids said together.

AURORA QUEEN OF SNOWS & BOREAS REX

Grandpop continued, "I created this junior treasure hunt because I want to remind you all of the mystery, fun, and magic of the Winter Carnival— and that it can be treasured by everybody, at any age. In fact, the kids in Saint Paul are the most important part of carrying on the Winter Carnival's spirit of Wonder."

The kids exchanged excited glances. Wonders was the word the flags had spelled. It all made sense now!

"But what I'm most proud about," Grandpop said with a warm smile. "Is that you solved the mystery using the seven values. They're what make Saint Paul a place that even King Boreas knew was special! Kindness, Humility, Respectfulness, Honesty, Generosity, Empathy, and Gratitude—these are things you each carry inside you, and if we remember to celebrate these gifts, Saint Paul will always be a place of magic, whether it's winter, summer, spring, or fall."

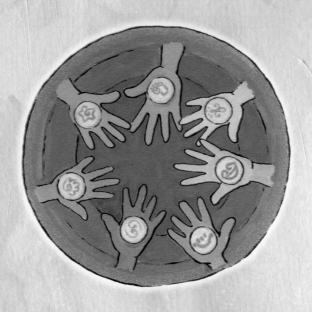

"I'll carry my coin in my pocket, always!" promised Joey.

"Me too!" Anika said.

Then came the chorus of replies from each of the other friends.

"Me three!"

"Me four!"

"Me five!"

"Me six!"

"Me seven!"

Anika smiled at her friends, and knew that these coins would always be a special reminder of the memories they made together in the winter of second grade.

Their treasure hunt had come to a close. But as the kids bundled themselves up to head for home, they got one last surprise. Big, plump snowflakes were coming down from the sky like a zillion downy feathers. The friends all danced around happily!

"Look at all this snow!" Anika said as she and Grandpop stood outside with her friends.

"I think this means the Saint Paul Winter Carnival will be extra perfect this year!"

About the Author

Kris Haslund is an educator with over forty years of experience, with a M.A. and Educational Specialist in Gifted Education. She loves teaching kids of all ages how to use their creative thinking powers to benefit our world.

Any spare time finds Kris up North hiking, boating, and cross-country skiing along Lake Superior. She is an avid gardener and traveler, and appreciates creative "good things" like musical performances, plays, art, and puppetry. She loves to read and shares her therapy dog, Legacy, at schools and libraries, where kids read books to her.

This is Kris' first book, and she has many more bubbling around in her imagination!

About the Illustrator

Sara Weingartner loves the winter, just like Boreas Rex, but gets to escape the cold to paint in her warm, cozy home studio. She believes that if everyone in the world takes the values in this story to heart, the whole world would be FILLED with WONDER, and oh, what a magical place this world could be. Sara lives in Minneapolis, Minnesota, with her husband and two kids. To see more of Sara's work, please visit www.creativesouldesign.com.

Autographs

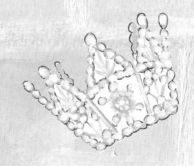

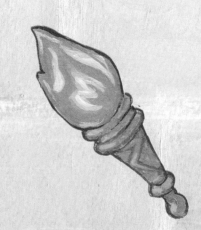

Autographs